The War on Cash

How Governments and Banks are Killing Cash and What You Can Do to Protect Yourself

By: Andrew Moran

About the Author

Andrew Moran is the Economics Correspondent at Liberty Nation.
He is also a commodities and foreign exchange news writer at
EarnForex.com. His work has been seen on CNS News, Zero
Hedge, The Mises Institute, Digital Journal, Economic Policy
Journal, and many more. He also runs a YouTube channel called
Think Liberty.

Introduction

As a member of the millennial generation, many of my fellow peers find it strange that my wife and I pay for most things in cash. Every Friday, we take out the necessary cash that will help cover our costs - groceries, coffee shop, dollar store, etc. - for the next seven days. We are by no means terrible with money, but it is always nice to have the money in your hand, and you don't have to worry about fraud, the payment systems not working, or losing your debit or credit card.

We have to use a Visa to pay for something we purchase on Amazon, but for most of the stuff we acquire in person we use cash. If we don't have enough cash on us to buy something then we simply don't buy it. We will wait or not buy it at all – the longer you wait, the better the odds of just forgetting about it and saving some dough.

Cash is a very good instrument. It would be nice if the cash in our wallets would be backed by something tangible, but cash is something that is always good to have in a wallet, in a safe, in a vehicle, or somewhere it can be accessed in case of an emergency or unexpected expense.

My grandmother, who lived during the Nazi occupation of Austria, always avoided banks as much as she could. She never used credit cards, checkbooks, or any alternative to cash. Even when it came to saving her money, paying bills or balancing the books, she used envelopes and special parts around the house. She would always use cash for everything.

For consumers born after the 1970s or 1980s, this would seem like an alien concept.

Many of our friends chuckle that they could never live without their Visa. And, yes, there are plenty of benefits to using a credit card, such points, rewards, or cashback, which are great when you make large purchases. But for the most part, cash is king in our household.

Has society stuck to the piece of wisdom that cash is king?

We are diverging from this sage advice.

Chapter 1

Brother, Can You Spare Some Legal Tender?

Cash, also known as money in physical form, is defined as legal tender that can be used to pay for goods, services, and debts. Legal tender is a form of payment that can meet financial obligations. In a rudimentary manner, cash is the simplest and most widely accepted form of payment today – well, depending on where you conduct your commerce.

Cash is derived from the Old Persian term "karsha," which means "a unit of value equivalent to one cash coin."

For years, businesses just wanted their customers to pay with cash because credit cards can be declined, debit cards can be costly for the merchant and checks can bounce. With cash, however, it does not require anything else other than exchanging it for goods and services and placing it in a cash register, wallet or safe. This has greatly changed in recent years due to the innovation in the payments industry (this is something we will explore in great detail).

Cash has had a very rich and diverse history, and has been used since markers provided goods and services. Whether it was a civilization using coins derived from precious metals (gold, bronze or silver) or a civilization relying on a commodity (salt or sugar) weight, cash has been at the forefront of commerce for thousands of years. Historians say the first use of cash can be found during the reign of Cyrus II of Persia, or Cyrus the Great, after a banking system was established in addition to credit and checking organizations.

Of course, today, cash comes in the form of paper that is not backed by anything. This is referred to as fiat money. Paper money can be traced back to the eighteenth or nineteenth century when the value of paper money was defined by the government's backing of a currency. Indeed, gold bugs, libertarians, and Austrian economists vehemently oppose this practice because it can lead to inflation in the money supply, a rise in prices, a decrease in the currency's purchasing power, and bigger government.

From the U.S. $100 banknote (Benjamin Franklin) to the Canadian $100 bill (Robert Borden), cash has always been referred to as king, hence the famous expression. But with each passing day, we begin to question that old adage due to the evisceration of cash, or at least attempts to by the establishment elites.

Cash plays a big part in emergencies. When you are stuck in the middle of nowhere with a dead car battery, cash is your only friend because it can, for instance, pay for tow trucks. When the power is out in your neighborhood, city or region (anyone remember the summer of 2003?), cash is the only thing that will be accepted for water, food and other important supplies.

Is it any wonder people place dollars, pounds, and euros in their safes next to their precious metals, jewelry, and bonds? They don't put credit or debit cards in their safes.

Heck, even when there was a gold standard, consumers could simply leave their gold or silver with a financial institution in exchange for banknotes. These banknotes would be redeemable in gold or silver. This allowed consumers to pay for items without having to lug around 10 ounces of gold on their backs, in their hands or in their purses.

The concept of cash is great. It allows us to conduct our businesses without the peeping authorities snooping on our every transaction. It helps us to have enough cash to cover an emergency. It facilitates us in fighting negative interest rates (more on that later). Indeed, cash, like gold and silver, sticks it to the man. Cash is a symbol of telling the government: Leave me the heck alone.

Chapter 2

It's All About the Data

In certain parts of the world, private businesses are required to accept cash as a method of payment. Although some laws are lax for companies to develop their own payment policies, governments are gradually moving away from this mandatory requirement. And consumers don't seem to mind.

Depending upon where you look, consumers are either fully adamant in transitioning away from cash and using mobile technology or apprehensive in parting with physical cash. For the most part, consumers are content with using their mobile devices and credit cards to make both big and small purchases. Whether it's their morning latte, weekly grocery shopping trip or a brand new winter coat, customers can expect a questionable look from the cashier if you're paying with cash. It is just become so common that the general public pays with plastic or mobile phone apps that a customer service representative has to take a double take by the method of payment.

When perusing the data, it provides a fascinating insight into cultural differences. In the United States, cash is king. In Asia, cash has taken a back seat to the latest trends in consumer payment options. In Europe, governments and banks are insisting on a cashless society while the people are divided and aren't exactly as keen as the public leaders.

There is very little argument in the concept that financial institutions, politicians and state bodies would prefer to impose a cashless society. However, if the policymakers were persistent in crafting such a landscape then the only way of achieving this venture is to win over the population. And this is gradually working.

Indeed, it seems like Baby Boomers and perhaps even older Generation Xers are the only hesitant people when it comes to abolishing cash. But once the millennials (those born between 1980 and 2000) and Generation Zers (those born after 2001) take over businesses, marketplace and government offices then things will likely be very different.

The younger generations just don't like ideas that seem antiquated, and this includes banking, checkbooks and cash. These are all boring and tedious vestiges of the last 100 years.

You'll always know someone who is, let's say, 23 years of age who will concede to the fact that they haven't step foot inside a banking branch since they opened an account. Some may not even have had to walk inside a branch thanks to Internet banks, including Tangerine, Ally Bank, or eQ Bank.

Bloomberg News had a report in November 2015 explaining that millennials have ditched the big banks and have gone local with their money. According to an Accenture Plc study, consumers banks saw a five percent increase in the number of account holders between 18 and 34, while the big banks saw millennials customers dip by 16 percent. Overall, the hip, tech-savvy generations are destroying conventional items, and cash may be on their hit list next.

So, where do the consumers stand on cash? Let's take a look at the numbers to find out.

United States

All of the data from the last two years suggest the same thing: Americans are relying on physical money. Cash is king to the minds of most American and Canadian spenders. It's safe, convenient and accepted pretty much everywhere. Surprising, isn't it? Despite banks and credit card companies hoping, North America transforms into a cashless utopia, we haven't arrived there yet.

A July 2015 survey by BlackHawk Network, a payment solutions firm, discovered that

93 percent of United States respondents reported having paid with cash in transactions in the last 12 months. What about checks and debit cards? Sixty-eight percent reported having used them for a transaction. Sixty-two percent said they have utilized PayPal. The remainder of the survey participants noted they used MasterCard or Visa gift cards (45 percent) and Apple Pay or Google Wallet (14 percent).

It is not a protest against technological trends as the reason for the overwhelming use of cash. It is just that it is convenient. Ninety-three percent of respondents listed cash as being the most convenient, though credit cards came in a close second with 92 percent.

Other studies support the same trend in the U.S.

Walker Sands, a marketing research firm, found that a majority (56 percent) feel cash is the safest form of payment. This is followed by 38 percent of U.S. consumers who believe credit cards are the safest. Consumers are ostensibly worried about their security and privacy when using mobile payments, and the unfamiliarity and paucity of confidence contributes to those fears. Ultimately, cash offers a better way to protect your vulnerable personal information than credit cards, mobile payment options or virtual currencies. Americans may like to pay with cash, but they certainly don't carry too much around.

A study by the Boston Federal Reserve's Consumer Payments Research Center said Americans carry an average of $56, a very small amount. Twenty-two percent of Americans carry a minimum of $100, and just five percent have a $100 banknote in their wallet.

All of the reports in the U.S. point to one fact: American consumers aren't the ones steering the country into a cashless society.

Canada on the other hand...

Canada

What about Canada? Any observer would conclude that Canadians are the same way. Not necessarily.

A May 2015 report from the Bank of Canada (BoC) informed everyone that Canadians are shunning cash in favor of plastic. Researchers do confirm that the Great White North is still far away from being a cashless society, but bit by bit, transaction by transaction, payment by payment, Canadians are gradually reaching that point.

"Many Canadians are still using cash for payments, especially for small-value transactions," the central bank wrote in the report. "Cash use in terms of volume has fallen, while the cash value share has remained relatively constant. This decrease is partly due to the increased use of payment innovations, such as contactless cards and stored-value cards, that compete with cash in terms of ease of use for small-value transactions."

The BoC's quarterly examination of trends and issues found a few interesting numbers between the years 2009 and 2013. There was a 10 percent decline of cash in the number of retail transactions, while there was a 31 percent increase. Debit card use fell to 21 percent.

Studies are backing up the central bank's claims, too.

An online study of 1,000 people by processing payments company Moneris found that more than three-quarters (77 percent) of Canadian consumers preferred to make purchases with a debit or credit card. The most important statistic from that study: 65 percent reported to never making payments with cash.

With credit card companies installing the tap option – you simply tap your credit card against a payment system to complete your purchase - this could mean the end of cash in the coming decades.

"I think we're at a point where you don't need cash for most of what you need to do today," Rob Cameron, chief product and marketing officer for Moneris, told The Canadian Press. "I do think people will continue to use cash because it's been around so long.... But this growth in contactless (payments using credit cards or mobile apps) I think is going to lead towards that end of cash." Canadians are more inclined to pick up their smartphones and credit cards from their pockets than cash.

Europe

Scandinavia is quickly becoming the epicenter of all cashless societies. It is leading the global trend of scrapping cash. Authors, bloggers, and journalists have regularly penned articles and white papers about how Scandinavia, particularly Sweden, Norway and Denmark, are transforming into a cashless paradise, an electronic oasis.

Credit Suisse wrote that in this region of Europe "if you have to pay in cash, something is wrong." This European region relies on cash for just six percent of all transactions.

Sweden has been described as the most cashless destination on Earth.

In fact, Stockholm's street magazine vendors aren't asking for random people on the street for some spare change. How come? They accept cards instead! The homeless are given portable card readers to take virtual payments. Publishers the newspaper say their sellers couldn't sell as many copies because people, despite their interest, didn't have any spare change on them.

So, the owners came up with a perfect solution: offer digital payment solutions.

"We didn't know how it would turn out, or whether people would be reluctant to give their credit card information to a homeless person," Pia Stolt of Situation Stockholm, the street paper sold by homeless vendors in Sweden's capital, told the London Guardian. "Swedes are pretty trusting and we're used to embracing new technology so this was the perfect solution. The cashless society campaign we're seeing in Sweden is definitely a good move as far as we are concerned – it's unstoppable."

Have the results been good? Vendors' sales are up an astonishing 59 percent.

Eighty percent of all purchases in Sweden are down electronically. The next step is to increase that number to 100 percent. Niklas Arvidsson, Sweden's Royal Institute of Technology, says banks and merchants have been investing heavily into card payment systems since the

1990s so consumers have already been accustomed to it for a long time.

Cash fares on Stockholm buses are non-existent, the Abba Museum doesn't accept cash or coins and tax collection is performed digitally. Are you a tourist? Be sure to sign up for prepaid tickets or a mobile registered in Sweden to get around. At more than half of the nation's largest banks, zero cash is in the branch and cash deposits aren't accepted. Swedish bank vaults with cash are diminishing: in 2010 there were 8.7 billion kroner in notes and coins, but that number collapsed to 3.6 billion in 2015. ATMs are being dismantled in the hundreds all over Sweden. Cards reign supreme with close to 2.4 billion credit and debit transactions in 2013, up from 213 million in 1998. Of course, plastic is facing competition from mobile apps (we'll explore this in another chapter).

Indeed, cash is surviving in Sweden – seniors and refugees are making sure of that – and the Riksbank recently introduced brand new kroner currency notes and coins. But the decline in use will continue for the next 20 years.

Even with all of the trends and initiatives in Sweden, Denmark may have the advantage. The Danish government is debating whether or not to remove the mandatory requirement for retailers to accept cash as a method of payment. This means restaurants, clothing retailers and newspaper vendors may not be legally mandated to accept cash payments.

Is Scandinavia's excitement for all things cashless seeping into the economies of other European states? Yes and no.

The United Kingdom no longer views cash as king. Cashless payments have become more dominant than banknotes and coin, says a study by Payments Council. According to the survey, use of cash by consumers, businesses and financial organizations declined to 48 percent of all payments in 2014. The remaining 52 percent ranged from electronic transactions to debit card payments. Report authors project cash volumes to decrease by 30 percent by the year 2025.

The industry body notes that contactless and mobile payments and plastic are driving the move away from cash. This is the first time that unconventional payments have collectively overtaken cash and coins in history.

Simply put: Britons are showing their disdain for cash, while showing the love for digital services and automated transactions. In Germany, the data portray consumers on the opposite side. The home of Ludwig van Beethoven, the frankfurter, and the Rhine maintains consumers pay for everything in cash and are reluctant to accept credit cards.

A Federal Reserve report highlighted the fact that German wallets hold twice as much cash ($123) as consumers in the U.S., France, Australia or The Netherlands. Moreover, 80 percent of all transactions across Germany are completed in cash, and cash is even used for large transactions.

Meanwhile, the Bundesbank notes that more than half (53 percent) of all private purchases in the country are paid with cash, which is actually the highest of all advanced economies. In terms of transactions from vendors, that number soars to 79 percent, even though most Germans have debit and credit cards.

The reason for this is simple: Germans are frightened of fraud, being charged too much or having their personal information stolen from hackers.

Is Europe going cashless? It all depends on whom you ask, where you go and what you buy. It should be interesting to see what would happen to consumers when a power outage occurs or systems are down.

Asia

Are Asian consumers embracing contactless payments? The answer is a resounding, enthusiastic yes.

It is remarkable to realize how far the East Asian economies have come. When these states, from China to Japan, Singapore to Hong Kong, first welcomed capitalism and free markets, consumers would pay with cash and shop in brick and mortar stores. Today, it is paying with smartphones and buying stuff online.

RFi Group, a financial services consultant organization, released the results of a survey and concluded that Asian consumers are leading the way in contactless payments and are faster adopters of this technology than other consumers in developed markets.

Making payments with a tap of your credit card or the click of a digital wallet is a lot more common in Asia than anywhere else around the world. Singapore (45 percent), Taiwan (41 percent) and Hong Kong (32 percent) are beating out the global average of 26 percent when it comes to the number of consumers making a contactless or electronic payment.

In addition, consumers in China, Indonesia, Hong Kong, Vietnam and Singapore are the top markets where people can foresee a cashless society. Also, emerging markets, including China, Indonesia and Vietnam, have the greatest potential to tossing cash into the trash bin.

Researchers say that a highly-connected population, an immense smartphone penetration rate, a young demographic and a thriving middle class have all helped cash enter into the history books. People aren't even shopping in stores anymore. In Japan, the ecommerce penetration rate is an astounding 97 percent, which means close to everyone in the economic powerhouse shops online.

"Emerging markets have an advantage because there's no strong legacy of a traditional payment method so consumers seem more enthusiastic at the introduction of digital or mobile payments," Gerald Ferguson, general manager of RFi Group, told *CNBC*. "In places like Indonesia and China, it's a pure numbers game. They have a large population with a digitallyengaged younger generation that's more willing to accept different payment methods."

Unlike their Scandinavian counterparts, consumers aren't entirely using cash for everything. For low-value purchases, such as a cup of coffee or a newspaper, consumers would rather pay with cash. Thailand (75 percent), Malaysia (71 percent), Indonesia (69 percent) and

Singapore (65 percent) are in the top of global consumers using cash in this type of transaction.

Credit card payments, mobile payments, smartphone payments, and mobile app payments all continue to garner a greater share of the payments market. That said, millions of consumers – mostly those not in the millennial age group – all over the world continue to use cash for safety reasons, emergencies, or fears of fraud. Although it can be wise to pay with cash for smaller purchases, a substantial number of consumers would rather pay with a simple tap or a wave of plastic over a card reader. Merchants don't mind, though, as the studies continue to purport the benefits of focusing on electronic payments.

Community Merchants USA published an infographic that suggested greater card acceptance led to the following benefits:

An increase in impulse purchases.

A jump in the number of sales.

Faster checkouts reduce transaction times.

Customers are more likely to be loyal with offered rewards and promotions.

As time goes by, more and more merchants will have no other choice but to offer more diverse payment options. Who knows? Perhaps in the next decade, consumers will start paying with eye scans or heartbeats (we'll cover that in the next chapter).

The next time that you patronize a Starbucks or Tim Hortons coffee shop in New York

City, Toronto, Tokyo, or London, take a gander at the customers who are paying for a $1.50 coffee and $1.00 doughnut with their credit cards or mobile apps. Then compare that to the number of people who pay with cash or coins. You'll be amazed at the vast gap in both camps.

It is correct to conclude that a majority of consumers are adopting and encouraging a cashless existence. But what's troubling is the fact that consumers will have no other choice but to adapt to society's whims. Seniors are already struggling across Scandinavia and Asia.

What will happen if you don't want to participate in a cashless society?

Chapter 3

How Would You Like to Pay Today?

Payment technologies are being developed all the time. The digital payments revolution is unfolding before our eyes. The number of payment methods just continue to increase with each passing day. A simple search on Google News with the term "payment technology" will yield an incredible number of results showcasing the tech firms, credit card companies and other enterprises developing a piece of technology that helps further deleting cash from our arsenal of payment choices.

Everything from tapping your smartphone to paying with an eye scan, the question isn't if cash will soon be gone but when it will be a distant memory. Banks have already gotten themselves prepared with these new technologies, merchants are biding their time and consumers are accepting it without any hesitation.

Right now, those promoting digital payments put forward these benefits:

- Protecting consumers from fraud.

- Understanding consumer's journey to shopping.

- GLP: Globalization, localization and personalization.

- Maintaining data and storage.

- Maximizing the rules of payment.

- Providing an omnichannel payment experience.

Let's also not forget about the endless possibilities of big data. Oren Levy, CEO of Zooz, writes in an op-ed piece about the relationship between big data and payment solutions:

"Data intelligence offers retailers critical knowledge and insight into the customer payment process, enabling them to create the best checkout experience to meet customers' needs. Whether merchants are active online, in-store, or across channels; whether they target local shoppers or a global audience; and even whether they offer physical or digital goods, merchants can best guide their customers through the checkout process using data from customer interactions with the brand, ultimately maximizing business performance."

Payment technology innovation never sleeps. If you've missed out on the wave of developments in the last year or two alone then we've got you covered:

Digital Currencies

Cryptocurrencies like bitcoin, dogecoin, litecoin, mastercoin, and even RonPaulCoin are regularly generating headlines. This type of e-cash, as was once predicted by economist Milton Friedman, is being seen all over the Internet. Although governments and central banks have repeatedly warned consumers about the dangers of digital currencies, banks, including Goldman Sachs, are gradually introducing their own virtual currencies, or have at least started investing in businesses developing digital currencies.

ADS VeriChip is Skin Deep

Will humans be walking payment systems? Will they be cyborgs? Years ago, many newspapers had headlines "mark of the beast" when describing a new method of payment that would be implanted under the skin. VeriChip, a U.S.-based fim received approval to design a chip that was constructed with minuscule antennas and an indentification number. It would be implanted in the soft tissue between the thumb and index finger and detected by an RFID, or radio-frequency identification, scanner

A consumer would simply wave their hand across a payment scanner and that would be all. Many feared at the time that it would be a superb GPS tracking device for the government. Although the product has gone under the radar, it's returning to prominence due to the fact that all these different kinds of payment solutions are being brought to the marketplace.

Paying with Selfies & Fingerprints

MasterCard will soon let you pay with selfies and fingerprints. The credit card titan announced February 2014 that it will be replacing passwords with selfies and fingerprints to confirm consumers' identities. With this new feature, consumers can make payments online with a simple snap of a selfie and a fingerprint scan.

According to Ann Cairns, head of international markets for MasterCard, this kind of biometric payment has been trialled in the U.S. and The Netherlands, and will soon arrive to the shores of Great Britain.

"I think the whole biometric space is a great way of protecting yourself when you are doing payments," she said. "There are a whole range of biometrics that say 'I'm me, I'm making a payment' and it just makes the whole thing more secure."

The purpose behind this is that it would generate greater online sales since passwords are replaced with something a lot more convenient. Since most shoppers forget their passwords, spend around 10 minutes to reset their accounts and ultimately abandon their purchases, this method of payment may turn that around.

Look into My Eyes

It seems like something straight out of old science-fiction movies or spy novels. But paying with your eyes is becoming a common thing, at least over in East Asia.

Fujitsu has a new phone out called Arrows NX F-04G that allows users to access stored information using their eyes. You simply look into the phone's front-facing camera as the phone scans your eyes. This will allow users to store credit card data and then pay for online purchasing by just staring into the screen.

It's All in Vein

Quixter is a biometric system developed in Sweden (any surprise?). It enables consumers to make a transaction in mere moments. How? Quixter verifies a user's ID by scanning the vein patterns in their palm. Customers just have to play their hand over a device after they enter the last four digits of their telephone number.

Pay with the Flick of Your Wrist

Is searching for your credit card in your purse bothersome? How about scrounging for some spare change in your pockets? There's a new solution for that: paying with the flick of a wrist.

Barclaycard, a UK-based credit card, has introduced a bPay wristband, key fob and sticker that allows British consumers to pay with a simple tap of the wrist. This is just another evolutionary step in the world of contactless payments.

How would you even use such a device? It is not that complicated. You transfer money

from your bank account to a bPay digital wallet. In order to spend that dough, you hold the wristband close to a contactless reader. You can also check the balance by using a mobile app.

What's next? Paying with your heartbeat? Oh wait...

Using Your Heartbeat for a Latte

What's the key to safe digital payments? Your heartbeat of course! At least, that is how it is being marketed by the developers of Nyomi.

The Canadian-based startup Bionym has created a wearable device that readers a user's electrocardiogram, otherwise known as your heart rhythm, in order to very if your identification. Heart rhythms, like a fingerprint, are unique, and this wristband can serve as an ID verifier in all sorts of transaction situations.

"So, it authenticates your identity, and once it knows who you are you can use it for things like unlocking your devices, bypassing passwords and pins, including making payments," said Karl Martin, Bionym's CEO and co-founder.

Your Smartphone is Money

It is truly perplexing to think how far the smartphone has come. In the early days of the smartphone, the smartphone was only an Internet communicator. Today, the smartphone can pretty much do anything, including make payments. In fact, smartphones are leading the way when it comes to digital payments solutions.

Here is a brief list:

Technology juggernaut Google released Google Wallet in 2011. It's a mobile payment app that looks to replace your actual wallet as it stores all of your credit cards and gifts into your smartphone.

Visa unveiled payWave for Mobile, which acts as another contactless payment system with the goal of making transactions much faster. All you have to do is wave your smartphone in front of a contactless payment terminal and it's done.

EE, a digital communications firm, confirmed that its customers can use their smartphone to pay to ride on London's vast bus network.

Still getting paid by check? Don't have time to head to the bank? No sweat. All you have to do now is to take a picture of the check with your phone in order to deposit the funds into your bank account. It seems like all of the major banks are adopting this technology.

Smartphone apps. From Starbucks to Wal-Mart, it seems every company is embracing mobile apps to assist in paying for your order. Just download the app, scan your phone and the payment is complete.

No one can predict what's next when it comes to how you pay. It is constantly evolving.

The Beginning of the End for Plastic

Plastic has helped dissolved the centuries-old momentum of cash. Debit and credit cards have assisted in the resolve of cash's volition. For the last 50 years, Visa and MasterCard (does anyone use Discover anymore?) have aided and abetted in the displacement of cash as a primary payment of method all over the world.

But is the joke on plastic now? After looking at all of the latest trends occurring, one could make the emphatic statement that it's the beginning of the end for plastic. PayPal, ApplePay and Google Wallet are just some of the products helping rid the world of plastic cards. Large or small denomination payments, clothing or coffee, digital payments are eliminating the once dominant use of plastic.

If all of these tech innovations and breakthroughs entice customers then it will reduce the immense volumes of credit cards. At the same time, it would establish large-scale and long-term ramifications for many of the major retail financial institutions since its card business is a major facet of their customer relationships and overall revenues.

No wonder why so many of the large-scale banks are turning to mobile payments options, smartphone payment apps and technologies and all of the (crazy?) method payments, like heartbeats, veins and wrist bands.

Will plastic become as obsolete as cash in the next 20 years? It's possible. Just look at

JPMorgan Chase's year-end plan.

Later in 2016, JPMorgan Chase will install brand new, state-of-the-art ATMs that will enable customers to conduct their banking business, such as transferring money or paying bills, by using their mobile phones. You won't be required to use a card.

These first-generation ATMs will see clients access their money by typing in a code sent to their Chase mobile app. Future updates will consist of utilizing the client's smartphone's nearfield wireless communication to gain access to the bank account.

A 2015 study reported that banks will invest heavily into biometrics by the year 2020. Banks will use biometrics as the primary banking ID method for proving your identification, withdrawing money or accessing web-based services.

The once bright future of plastic is gradually being dimmed.

Chapter 4

Please, Sir, Tell Me More

Deutsche Bank CEO John Cryan predicted in January 2016 that cash will not survive another decade. Judging by this statement, it's debateable as whether he's jubilant or cautious.

After reading the plethora of reports, op-eds and studies, it would have you think that the banks, economists and financial analysts are leading the charge towards a cashless society.

They are driving the push toward an economy without banknotes and coins, and in its place are taps, smartphones and apps, whether you like it or not.

If you read what is written in columns and listen to what is being posited on national television, you would immediately conclude that everyone thinks having a society without cash and entirely dependent on electronic payment is the way to go. Considering that these individuals and institutions flood the airwaves and cloud the newspapers, it's easy to fall into that line of thinking.

The desire for a cashless economy, at least in Europe and the United States, has never been so ubiquitous then over the past year or so. It seems nearly every day a major bank is implementing a policy to make it harder to access your cash in the name of protecting ordinary citizens. It seems nearly every day some bright financial mind is arguing for the complete eradication of cash to stimulate the economy or to ensure the black market doesn't flourish.

One economist actually proposed in April 2015 of abolishing cash and taxing currency.

Citibank economist William Buiter put forward a proposal to end cash, impose a tax on currency and removed the fixed exchange between currency and central bank reserves and deposits. He argued that since interest rates are close to zero and the Federal Reserve can't print more money than it does and depositors are putting less of their cash in banks because of low rates. Consumers don't save, banks don't lend money out. This is otherwise known as the effective lower bound (ELB) on nominal interest rates.

The ELB exists because of cash that does not pay nominal rates. Consumers will not deposit money into a bank account that maintains a negative rate that essentially reduces your wealth. Therefore, cash allows people to avoid negative nominal rates. Buiter, who thinks the amount of money printed since 2008 isn't enough, suggested his ideas this would spur economic growth. He conceded that it is a controversial one, but notes that the arguments against his premise are weak.

The common arguments he outlined include:

- Abolishing currency would create change and change is resisted.

- Currency use is still high among low-income consumers.

- Governments and central banks would suffer from a loss of "seigniorage revenue."

- Eliminating currency would lead to a reduction in privacy and create government intrusion.

- Switching to electronic payment systems would produce security risks.

At the time the report was composed, most experts agreed that no such thing would happen. Why can't it happen, though? A lot of policymakers and bankers thought negative interest rates wouldn't take place, but look at Japan, Europe, and elsewhere. Also, a lot of economists are hopping on the Eviscerate Cash Now! bandwagon. Kenneth Rogoff, a professor of public policy and economics at Harvard University, declared in the Financial Times in 2014 that "paper money is unfit for a world of high crime and low inflation," adding "phasing out currency would address the concern that a significant fraction, particularly of large-denomination notes, appears to be used to facilitate tax evasion and illegal activity." One year later he garnered the support from one prominent British economist. Bank of

England (BOE) chief economist Andy Haldane told the Portadown Chamber of Commerce in Northern Ireland that in order to generate economic growth in the UK that perhaps it would be time to introduce negative interest rates and ban cash.

European Central Bank (ECB) President Mario Draghi, who adopted a zero-interest-rate-policy (ZIRP) and unleashed quantitative easing in 2014, told reporters that he has been mulling over the initiative of erasing the 500-euro banknote from circulation. He alluded to crime, which looks like the scapegoat for everyone promoting the move.

In February 2016, Larry Summers a Harvard economist, former United States Treasury

Secretary and ex-economic adviser to President Barack Obama, wrote a column in the Washington Post advocating for the end of the $100 bill.

"Harvard's Mossavar Rahmani Center for Business and Government, which I am

privileged to direct, has just issued an important paper by senior fellow Peter Sands and a group of student collaborators. The paper makes a compelling case for stopping the issuance of high denomination notes like the 500 euro note and $100 bill or even withdrawing them from circulation."

Summers further added:

"A global agreement to stop issuing high denomination notes would also show that the global financial groupings can stand up against 'big money' and for the interests of ordinary citizens." At around the same time, Trond Bentestuen, executive vice president at DNB, Norway's largest financial institution, spoke with a newspaper averring the virtues of eliminating cash. He alluded to such statistics as the Norges Bank being unable to account for 60 percent of the kroner in circulation. Like others before him, and surely those succeeding him, he cited money laundering schemes, the black market and street crime as reasons to forget cash.

"That means that 60 percent of money usage is outside of any control. We think much of it revolves around the black economy and money laundering," the banker said. "There are so many dangers and disadvantages associated with cash, we have concluded that it should be phased out."

The purported criminal activity is an excuse that dates back to 1970, a time when some say the war on cash officially began. This is what prominent economist Joseph Salerno writes:

"It all started really with the Bank Secrecy Act of 1970, passed in the US, which requires financial institutions in the United States to assist US government agencies in detecting and preventing money laundering. That was the rationale. Specifically, the act requires financial institutions to keep records of cash payments and file reports of cash purchases or negotiable instruments of more than $10,000 as a daily aggregate amount. Of course, this is all sold as a way of tracking criminals."

Finansrådet, a Danish finance industry lobbying group, supported the idea a few months prior. This time, the organization stated that it can save companies money on security and currency management, adding that businesses can take advantage of the latest payment solutions trends.

The world's biggest and most prominent newspapers and magazines have contracted the abolish cash fever. *The New York Times*, *The Wall Street Journal*, and *The Economist* have all published editorials and op-eds why exactly the world should go paperless. It is these scribes and columnists who have the alacrity to convey the messages of the elite, the globalists, and the statists.

According to these geniuses, if you are opposed to the idea of moving away from cash then you are a luddite, you lack the progressivism and triumphant wisdom unlike these munificent journalists.

Evidently, these adversaries of cash contend that criminals need large-denomination banknotes. And it is only these crusaders of justice who can save us all from the bad guys.

So, is this all talk without any actions backing it up? Not quite. Banks and central banks have started to implement policies that would limit cash.

As discussed in chapter two, Scandinavian financial institutions are eliminating ATMs, not accepting cash deposits and reducing the amount of cash they have in their vaults. But elsewhere around the world you're already finding the trends unfolding before your eyes.

Here are a few developments that have happened in recent months:

- Cash transactions of more than 1,000 euros will be banned in France.

- In Spain, cash transactions over 2,500 euros are no longer allowed,

- Italy has banned cash transactions of more than 1,000 euros.

- JPMorgan Chase is requiring customers to show photo ID when making cash deposits. It's also deterring customers from depositing large sums of cash by charging fees.

- State Street Corp. has started charging customers for large dollar deposits.

Bankrate.com posted a widely reported study that found U.S. banks have instituted record

ATM and checking account fees. The charges vary from city to city. For instance, you're more likely to pay higher ATM fees in Atlanta and New York ($5.15 and $5.03, respectively), while you'll pay smaller ATM fees in Philadelphia and Los Angeles ($4.29 and $4.28, respectively).

Overall, though, ATM fees are higher, checking account fees are higher, overdraft costs are higher and things like free account minimums are vanishing. Although higher fees aren't exactly direct capital controls, it is a form of a tax to access your own dough.

The reason for these drastic rate hikes is because banks have no other alternative in today's economy. It's becoming more and more expensive just to hold on, protect and to maintain your money.

Banks would greatly benefit from a cashless society because, for example, bank runs would be a thing of the past since there is no form of cash that isn't controlled by banks. But you would mostly be harmed in such a world. (we'll tackle this in the next chapter). The list of banks shying away from cash goes on. Cash is being taken behind the dumpster and killed off one central bank at a time, one financial institution at a time, one economist at a time.

***

Once again, it is the supposed smartest men in the room, the self-anointed intellectuals of our society that are coming up with the new rules on the fly. They're the ones dictating what we can or cannot do. They make the terms without our approval. You can't make certain transactions over a certain amount, you can't make certain deposits at a certain amount. It's becoming nothing but tommyrot.

Many will purport that banks are not to blame over these changes and the presented war on cash. They are only following the market trends and trying to combat government policies. In a way this is a correct assessment, but they're amplifying the transition. They are participants in the path to a cashless society.

Danish banks are not accepting cash deposits, the U.S. banks are requiring photo identification just to touch your own money and Norwegian banks are demanding an end to cash.

They don't have to do this, do they? They don't have to facilitate a cash ban, do they?

Banks are not victims. They're collaborators. And it's the economists who are putting these ideas into the minds of not just the banks but also the policymakers.

What is really interesting is that once again we are insouciant. We are not showing any temerity or spirit in combating this trend.

Chapter 5

Be Afraid. Be Very Afraid

It is as simple as this: Whether you like it or not, a cashless world is coming. The statists, the elite, the bankers, the central bankers, the economists, and all of the so-called brilliant minds are instituting such a society without your opinions. If you oppose this plan, then an International Monetary Fund (IMF) expert says to move ahead anyway.

Economic growth or preventing of fraud, the officials leading our world are coming up with any sort of excuse to make cash a distant memory.

You should be worried by a cashless world. Sure, you likely don't mind now because you still have cash as a payment of choice. But for how long? For how long can you carry a wallet with cash to pay for a pair of socks, a cup of tea or even your rent for that matter. Sweden,

Denmark and Norway's pursuit of a nation without cash is passing by the seniors and other groups on the margin.

Of course, there is more than just the paucity of choice as cause for concern. As we explore, a cashless world can permit those at the top to run roughshod on the general public. If you thought the banks, the politicians and the Federal Reserves of the world had an enormous amount of power today, just think what it would be like when they track every purchase you make, tax every transaction you have and diminish the wealth in those digits you have in your bank account.

Let's explore as to the precise reasons you should be frightened by a marketplace without cash.

Your Privacy is Gone

The move toward digits would eliminate anonymity.

Today, the authorities can track and monitor each purchase you make when you use a credit card, a debit card, a mobile payments app or any other non-cash payment option. By typing in a few codes, officials can determine what you eat for breakfast, how you spend your leisure time, and where you go to the movies.

Every time you tap, swipe or wave you leave a trackable trail behind.

All what governments and hackers can do is follow the digital dipped road.

Essentially, your privacy has been wiped away. Cash, like gold, is anonymous, and authorities can't track every banknote you spend - indeed, they can track when you withdrew cash from your bank account.

A cashless society is an attack on your privacy.

Similar to other government spying programs, some citizens will contend that they have nothing to hide so why should they be concerned? This is the wrong way to view the matter.

Your privacy is your right, it's a part of your liberty. By monitoring and tracking your commerce is a negation of your liberty. We all have a right to be left alone without being followed by a government body or a local authority, especially if we have not committed a crime or suspected
of illicit activities.

Big Brother is watching.

The Potential for Fraud is Immense

In addition to being concerned about privacy, you also have to be worried about facing fraud. The chances of experiencing fraud are a lot higher if pretty much the entire population is embracing electronic method of payment.

For a real-world example, all one has to do is look back a couple of years when an array of stores experienced a data breach and security infiltration. In late 2014, the U.S. government announced that more than 1,000 businesses, including Target, UPS, Jimmy John's and

Supervalu, had been the target of malicious malware. As the point of sales systems were infected with the malware, hackers stole millions of customers' credit and debit card information.

U.S. businesses and customers aren't the only ones prone to security breaches and personal theft. In early February 2016, close to 100,000 Britons had their names, addresses and bank information stolen and posted on a website. The list included consumers from China, Greece, Argentina, India, Taiwan,

Denmark, the Bahamas, Australia and Zimbabwe And such incidents are still occurring every single day, from Canada to New Zealand, from China to Great Britain.

What should be noted is that despite the surging number of data breaches, it's not driving consumers back to cash, says Douglas Ceto, CEO and President of CetoLogic, a provider of software and analytics solutions.

"In light of recent history, financial institutions should reconsider the notion of promoting card use for every transaction, no matter how small," explained Ceto in an op-ed piece. "For one thing, if more customers use cash, they will visit branches and ATMs more frequently. This will give banks a greater number of one-on-one customer interactions and cross-sell opportunities."

Although Sweden is pretty much the cashless capital of the world, it's also one of the top places for electronic fraud cases. According to a report from Sweden's Ministry of JUstice, the number of electronic fraud cases skyrocketed to 140,000 in 2014, which is more than double compared that in 2004.

It is easy to fathom: the more people using credit cards and smartphones, the greater the odds more people will be hacked.

Central Bank Policies - Fractional Reserve Lending & Subzero Rates

Since the economic collapse of 2008, the global economy has nor fully recovered. For the last decade or so, global economic growth has remained tepid. It ia not going anywhere, even though central banks have tried everything under the sun: money printing, stimulus, near-zero interest rates, and asset purchases.

One last bullet left in the arsenal of the central banks is subzero interest rates. This is when interest rates dip below zero percent. This policy is being tried all over the world by central banks, including in Japan, Sweden, Denmark, and Switzerland. ECB's Mario Draghi also rolled out this policy. Federal Reserve Chair Janet Yellen conceded that negative rates are on the table should an economic disaster transpire, while Bank of Canada Governor Stephen Poloz generated headlines when he said subzero rates could be introduced amid falling oil prices. The Bank of Japan (BOJ) is in negative, and the Swiss are paying for the privilege of lending to the banks as the Swiss National Bank (SNB) has dipped below zero.

It suggests a sign of desperation on the part of the central banks. They have run out of traditional policy options and have had to embrace unconventional monetary tools that will ultimately fail. The idea behind subzero rates is that consumers will spend money, the banks will lend more money out, and the economy will be stimulated.

Negative rates are the result when a central body – in this case a central bank – is in charge of manipulating and artificially reducing interest rates. If the market was in charge of interest rates then rates would never, ever go below zero. It is impossible.

The real, or natural, rate of interest cannott be negative. Interest rates are a function of the preference of consumers for present goods versus future goods. If one were to allocate any credence to negative rates then it would mean a consumer prefers less in the future to more in the present; you would rather have $50 today than $20 the next day. As the Mises Institute's Paul Martin Fos writes, this is "voodoo mathematics" on the part of mainstream economists. What do negative rates mean for you as a saver? You will be charged for just having money in your savings account. The money in your savings will be eroded, not just by inflation but by the bank decreasing the available amount. Financial institutions have to perform this dire measure because it costs them way too much to hold onto your cash - it should be noted, however, that some banks in Switzerland have avoided doing this but how much longer can they hold out?

The unintended consequences are astronomical.

World-renowned economist Walter Block tears apart the premise behind negative rates:

"A basic principle of Austrian economics is that the originary rate of interest (the rate of discount of future goods compared to present, otherwise identical, goods) can never be negative. The reason for this arises not because capital is productive, nor out of man's psychology. Nevertheless, in spite of the foregoing, there are many benighted souls who insist upon the possibility of a negative rate of originary interest. They are continually discovering cases which 'prove' their conclusion. The number of such examples has reached such proportions that it seems advisable to take account of them in a systematic way. Accordingly, this paper is devoted to classifying them in a manner that makes the most intuitive sense: in accordance with the economic errors which are necessarily committed in their very statements."

Economies cannot be stimulated in a negative rate environment. Economists expect miracles with this policy tool. But one just has to look to Sweden, where consumers are hiding their kroner in microwaves, under the mattress, and anywhere else where they shield their wealth from the hands of bureaucrats and bankers.

One other thing: Banning cash help props up the unstable fractional reserve banking system.

Unfortunately, when you live a cashless state, you don't even have the choice to place your cash under the mattress. Therefore, your wealth will deteriorate as long as the central banks maintain negative rates.

Another Case of Taxes

Death and taxes are the only permanent facets of society, said one influential mind years ago.

The amount of taxes consumers everywhere pay is flummoxing. Income taxes, sales taxes, liquor taxes, cigarette taxes, property taxes and the list goes on and on - as previously mentioned, one economist wants to even pass a tax on currency.

Since the financial crisis, there is one segment of the economy that is growing at a rapid rate: The underground economy. At this term, you may conjure up images of men in black coats selling stolen watches, drugs and/or weapons. However, the 21st century version of the underground economy consists of waiters hiding their tips, contractors getting paid in cash and freelancers underreporting their incomes to the taxman.

All of the above is able to transpire because they get paid in cash. Without cash, all of these transactions would be taxed. Voila! That gives politicians, bureaucrats and tax collectors a stellar idea!

Meanwhile, in some parts of the world, the crony fix is in. Greece announced in early 2015 that it would be imposing a surcharge for all cash withdrawals from bank accounts in order to prevent citizens from taking their money out of the banks.

In a cashless society, any and all transactions can be taxed without hesitation or avoidance. This has worked out quite well in the cashless Scandinavia where tax collection rates have swelled dramatically in recent years.

No wonder why someone like 2016 U.S. presidential candidate Bernie Sanders wants to emulate Denmark, Sweden, and Norway so badly! He wants to tax you to pay for his socialism.

Mandatory Use of the Banks

In a world without cash you will have no other choice but to use a financial institution.

According to a 2014 World Bank Global Findex report, the number of "unbanked"

individuals stands at two billion. The international organization was sure to point out that there has been a great surge in the number of adults who have signed up for a bank account. But it's still a hefty number

In the U.S. alone, one in nine households does not have a checking account. When delving further into the data, more than one-quarter (28 percent) of households with incomes less than $15,000 do not have a bank account at all.

Once a country becomes cashless, you will have to sign up for a bank account in order to buy a product, use a service, take a bus and to go about your day-to-day business. The banks will enjoy this; the consuming public will be required to join a bank. It's a dream come true: millions of more people will have to enter the system and be charged for every time a customer swipes a card, taps a piece of plastic or flicks their wrists.

Yes, financial institutions will have to compete with other brands when it comes to products, but just the fact that consumers have to sign up for a bank is astounding.

The Start of the Bail-in Program

Michael Snyder of *End of the American Dream*, a blog covering the economic calamities transpiring all over the world, opines something even more unscrupulous:

"In addition, there would be absolutely no escaping the bank bail-ins that are coming in Europe. If there was no way to pull your money out of the system, there would be no way to avoid the kind of theft that has now been institutionalized by European authorities."

Wait a minute. Bail-ins? Yes, bail-ins.

Former Bank of Canada Governor Mark Carney revealed to a Thomson Reuters audience

in 2013 that an international organization of bankers are devising a global bail-in effort. A bailin is when a bank has to look for money from within to solve a financial crisis, which is the opposite of a bailout when money originates from an outside source, such as the government.

This led to speculation that Canada's banks would be participating. Nothing has happened at the time of this writing, but if it's going on in Europe then it's only a matter of time before it starts to unfold in the U.S. and Canada.

Bank bail-ins have already occurred in Cyprus and Portugal.

Portugal's troubled Novo Banco covered its billion-dollar deficit by essentially stating that more than $2 billion in bonds were null and void. Over in Cyprus, bondholders and depositors with more than 100,000 euros in their accounts took a haircut.

Some politicians have declared these moves as successes. Jeroen Dijsselbloem, the Dutch head of the Eurogroup of finance ministers, hinted that bail-ins could serve as a template for future rescues.

Yikes!

It should be noted that he quickly retracted his statement after it received heavy criticisms.

Nonetheless, anxieties of depositors and bondholders remain heightened over in Europe, which is starting to travel to the borders of North America. And who could blame them? No one.

You Will Conform

Silicon Valley, Big Tech, and the big banks have colluded in recent years to go after anyone who dares violate groupthink. Should you have a different opinion that does not confirm to leftist dogma, then you become the enemy of many of the companies we rely upon. This is a dangerous trend.

More people are relying on digital tools, online platforms, and tech payment systems to earning a living or pay their bills. From Patreon to PayPal, millions are using these services. One day, if these firms decide that they no longer want to do business with you, then you are in a danger zone.

Conspiratorial? If it were that simple.

In addition to shadow bans and biased algorithms, conservatives are finding that it is becoming harder to earn revenue on their content, fundraise, or make a living.

In recent years, YouTube has started to demonetize popular conservative personalities, including Steven Crowder and Mark Dice. This prompted many to turn to alternative platforms to generate revenue from fans, primarily Patreon. But Patreon has started to crack down on users who receive monthly donations from supporters, some of whom aren't even right-leaning but hold different views that the thought police do not like. These names include Laura Southern, Milo Yiannapolous, Carl Benjamin, and

Sargon of Akkad. Major users, like Jordan Peterson, Dave Rubin, and Sam Harris, have quit the platform on principle.

Others have tried out Stripe and PayPal for financial backing, but they have withdrawn their services because these individuals ostensibly violate their rules.

Even banks are participating in this abhorrent practice. Chase Bank, for example, has been quietly shutting down conservative accounts.

Yes, these are private companies and can do what they like, but it is still a warning sign about why we still need cash and an offline option.

Chapter 6

War on Cash: Or, How I Learned to Not Worry and Love Cash

As the world inches closer to a cashless society, you may have already decided that you do not want to be an active participant. You prefer to use cash to plastic, you prefer coinage to heart beats. It may indeed seem like an impossible task to protect yourself from being sucked into a marketplace without cash. But the only way to shield you and your family from a globe of plastic, taps and swipes is to start right now.

There are plenty of ways to initiate a plan to defend yourself from be a victim of government following, tracking and monitoring every transaction you make. It's true that you have to take baby steps right now, but you slow and steady wins the race.

We shall look at what methods you can incorporate into your daily lifestyle so you will not be coerced into using eye scans, selfies, and veins to pay for your cup of coffee, pair of pants, or vintage Tom Jones records.

Here are ways to protect yourself in the war on cash.

The Hoarder, or How I Learned to Love Cash

Our grandparents were part of a generation that kept a lot of their money at home. Their cash would be stuff under the mattress, socked away in drawers, placed in safes and even stored inside of a door. Even our parents realized that it would be wise to have at least some dollars available at your disposal at home in the event of an emergency.

What about today's generation? Are they storing their money under the mattress and in the freezer? Since the economic collapse of 2007 and 2008, the answer would be yes. But don't tell any financial managers or investment groups because they hate the idea (of course they would).

According to a 2015 survey by American Express, more than one-quarter (29 percent) of Americans say they are keeping some of their banknotes and coins at home. Of those respondents who are hoarding cash at home, more than half (53 percent) are hiding it in a clandestine location. Surprisingly, millennials are the most adamant of sleeping on their cash.

More than two-thirds (67 percent) of millennials are saving their cash outside of a bank account.

Why are consumers hiding cash in their living quarters? They are anticipating financial emergencies, and this is one way to be prepared for an unforeseen event, like a broken refrigerator, a flat tire or a leak in your faucet. Others are also using the technique to ensure they're following their budgets, which is also known as the envelope method.

Here are four ways to start hoarding cash at home:

Take between one and three percent of your monthly earnings and leave it at your place of residence

If you have leftover cash at the end of the week save it at home.

As part of your monthly savings goal, subtract five percent of the total amount and store it in a safe, container or whatever else you use to hoard your cash.

Never store large bills at home; ensure you have smaller denominations.

No one will argue that there are safety concerns involved, but it takes a bit of cleverness and common sense to store money at home.

Security expert Todd Morris, founder and chief executive of BrickHouse Security, warned *CNBC* in 2015 that the drawback of hoarding cash at home is that burglars know where all the hotspots are. This can prove dangerous not only to your financial health, but also to the safety of you and your family.

"Burglars definitely know certain places to look, like the bottom of your sock drawers, and underneath your drawers, where it's easy to tape an envelope [of cash]," he said. "If you think about your house and you know where things are, you can think about some places where people wouldn't look."

Whether you want to hide it from burglars, the taxman or Bernie Sanders, here are several tips to safely store your cash at home:

- **Book**: Inside a random book on your bookshelf, particularly a book that most people aren't likely to read, such as a Paul Krugman book.

- **Lettuce Storage**: You can actually buy a storage that looks like a head of lettuce. So purchase one, store some of your cash in there and leave it in your fridge.

- **Empty Aspirin Bottle**: Instead of just chucking away that empty pill bottle, store your cash inside. Simply roll up your cash with a rubber band and leave it inside the bottle in your medicine cabinet.

- **Litter Box**: Do you have cats? Don't let that litter box be used just for your cats to release themselves in. Grab an envelope, put your cash inside and tape it to the bottom of the box.

- **Flashlight**: It's likely that your flashlight died out. Rather than throwing it in the garbage, take the batteries out and put some cash inside. None is the wiser!

- **Dirty Socks**: In the event of a burglary, nobody would want to touch or smell your stinky gym socks. So grab a pair of disgusting, foul and grotesque socks and put your money inside. Be sure to tuck away those socks in the bottom of your drawer.

One common piece of advice presented by safety experts is to hide your cash in one place. This prevents you from losing your cash savings. In other words, unless you have a stellar memory, leave your cash in one location in your home. Don't scatter it in your backyard, basement, vehicle and bedroom.

A Penny a Day Keeps the Government Away

There's an old saying: a penny found is a penny earned.

A couple of years ago, John Stossel, the former host of Fox Business Network's Stossel, did a segment with pennies. He scattered them all over the sidewalk to see if anybody would pick up the array of coins with Abraham Lincoln's face. Nobody did. Pennies may be dying a slow death all over the world - Canada has gotten rid of them, ditto for Australia and some in the United States are pushing for the similar thing. The copper cents may die, but change is very much alive.

It is always a good idea to have a jar of coins, whether they're nickels, dimes or quarters.

If they are old then that is even better. For instance, if the dimes you have in your possession were made before the 1970s then they have some silver inside of them. If the pennies hidden away in your closet were minted prior to the 1960s then they are 90 percent copper.

Many financial institutions now have a change machine where you deposit your unwanted change into cash free of charge. It is a tremendous service that makes the days of packaging your change into round containers obsolete. However, you shouldn't be so dismissive with your change. Keep them, at least most of them anyway.

Here are ways to start collecting your pennies and dimes today:

- If you receive change following a transaction then drop that change into a jar.

- Notice a penny or a nickel on the street? Pick it up and keep it.

- Always wait for change after your transaction. Some people don't think it's worth it to wait for 13 cents in change after buying a coffee, but it really is! It all adds up.

- Don't have enough change at home? Exchange your banknotes for coins.

During a purchase, don't give the cashier the exchange change. For example, if your purchase comes to $12.34, don't give them that exact amount of change. Instead, just hand over $15 or $20 and keep that change.

Many people who have started to collect change at home have begun to feel more secure at home. There is something reassuring about the fact that you have $20 in change at home, even if you're going to use some of that money to buy yourself a coffee on a Wednesday evening.

You've Caught the Gold Bug

If you have yet to be infected with the gold bug then you should be; own gold, silver, copper, platinum and palladium. Precious metals are not only a great investment to protect your wealth from currency debasement and price inflation, but it is also a superb technique to shield yourself from the war on cash.

Gold has been used as money for eons. The yellow metal is attractive because it's durable, has intrinsic value, is easily transportable and has been used all over the world for thousands of years. Moreover, unlike fiat paper money, the state can't obliterate the value of your precious metals. Central banks also can't erode the value of your bullion holdings through the power of negative interest rates. And, most importantly, unlike the digital cash in your bank account, it's impossible for the government to confiscate your precious metals with a few keyboard keys.

Owning physical gold or silver is essential to not only survive and thrive economic downturns, but to also prevent yourself from becoming a victim to the global war on cash.

You can own coins, rounds, bars, or any other type of gold.

As long as it is real, you're as good as gold.

Chapter 7

I've Got the Power

Depending upon where you are in the world, you are likely seeing more and more of your fellow consumers buy their lattes with their smartphones, purchase their cereal with a tap, and even acquire a sandwich with a flick of a wrist. You see, there are just so many contactless payment solutions available for everyone that a declining number of people are using cash.

A cashless society may not be such a big deal to the general public. They are already embracing credit cards, Apple Pay, and their fingerprints. So, why they should be concerned about this global transition to a cashless world?

Although your friends, families and colleagues are unimpressed about your warnings of the dangers of going digital, contactless and cashless, you are extremely worried about the implications. Well, if you truly are then there's one thing you can do: fight back against the system.

The fact is is that so many of us are frightened of contradicting the status quo. We are petrified of being given dirty looks if we pay with cash or scared that our date will have second thoughts if he or she notices you picking up a dime on the street. We should not be so concerned with others' perceptions related to our habits.

This is a part of the reason why we hardly ever fight back: Other people don't then why should we? This is the wrong way to think. How can one engage in combat in this war to eviscerate banknotes? It is simple: embrace those $5, $10, $20, $50, and even $100 bills.

Here are ways to fight back the next time you start your trip to the grocery store, coffee shop or movie theater:

Pay with Cash

Paying with a credit card has become attractive because it simplifies transactions, offers us rewards and an unlimited supply of instant gratification.

But this Faustian trick is exactly that: a trick. Just because a credit card offers you one percent cash back rewards, it doesn't mean you won't be charged 20 percent if you accidentally miss a payment. Just because you have $15,000 at your disposal, it doesn't mean that you can spend like a drunken sailor, or a politician.

In other words, you should begin to conduct a large portion of your purchases with cash.

Whether it's a buck or $100, resist the temptation to whip out your American Express,

MasterCard or Visa to make the payment. Instead, take out that piece of paper in your wallet and complete the transaction that way.

You see, one way to change the market is to use your wallet to do so. The market listens.

Let's face it: if a payment solutions provider notices that 85 percent of its consumers are avoiding contactless payments and continue to use cash then they will cease developing technologies that aid the evisceration of cash. It's simple economics.

The government and central banks will have to listen, too. If enough consumers demand cash from their financial institutions then they will have to maintain large cash reserves, high withdrawal limits and other policies that are cash-friendly as opposed to an enemy of cash.

Getting Paid in Cash

It seems near impossible to get paid in cash today. With automatic deposits, checks and

PayPal, no one receives their weekly, bi-weekly or monthly pay in crisp $20 bills. It is all electronic now. The days of being handed cash and a receipt are long gone.

The benefit of working for yourself or being a contractor is that you could always get paid in cash. You could offer a discount or some other special benefit if you get paid with banknotes as opposed to an electronic transfer or a check.

The same benefit, however, cannot be extended to a full-time employee working at a corporation. But there is a solution: Withdraw a specific portion of that paycheck in cash. Let's say you were given a $1,000 paycheck so then why can't you withdraw $500 of that in cash to pay for your groceries, coffees and trips to the shopping mall? The answer is you can!

Avoiding the Latest Technologies

We all want to be a part of something big, something revolutionary. We all want to embrace a technology that is going to change the world. It's why we all adopted smartphone technology as opposed to maintaining a flip phone or a rotary phone in our homes.

When it comes to making payments and the war on cash, the best remedy of resistance is to refrain from buying into the hype of taps, swipes, eye scans, heartbeats and fingerprints. To assist in discouraging payment solutions firms from creating even more of this kind of technology and to help in dissuading businesses from installing these payment solutions, we should not use it.

That is the only way that we can send the message to the free market. Indeed, if we continue to lambast the war on cash but then install a new mobile application to make a purchase quicker and easier, then it is a futile endeavor. Bashing a cashless society but then buying into the hype is not going to solve anything. It will just exacerbate the issue at hand.

Moving forward, avoid these new payment technologies as much as you can and just use cash for all of your transactions.

Final Thoughts

It is said that once cash is outlawed then the holders of cash become the outlaws. Only time will tell as to whether or not cash is prohibited and illegal. Governments want cash gone because it wipes away the black market (at least somewhat), it makes it easier to tax every transaction, and it becomes simpler to follow and trace your every move. Banks want cash to be nothing more than an antiquated tool because then you will have no other choice but to insert yourself into the vast financial system. Central banks and economists want the obliteration and evanescence of cash because then it allows them to conduct even more dangerous but perceived propitious monetary experiments. The average consumer does not wish to be obstreperous because he will welcome any new technological trend that can help him avoid being inconvenienced at the local coffee shop, clothing vendor, or bookstore.

Years after this book is released into the public realm, there will be far more developments made by tech startups in the field of digital payment solutions. Vainglorious central banks and governments will have enacted even more whacky policies. Banks will have installed new policies and gotten rid of old ones. Consumers, meanwhile, will have adopted and adapted to all of the above. The war on cash is a relatively new battle perpetrated and fought by the self-anointed, the supposed intellectuals in every room of government, university lecture hall, or bank branch. But there is no resistance being put forward to fight back against this trend. It's for the simple fact that many consumers don't mind the idea of paying with a thumbprint or using their smartphone. We may think that we have a choice in society. But the powers at hand have declared the war on cash, and they are making the choice for you: We are going cashless; commerce has gone mobile. You have no say in the matter.

It has been long argued that the only way to let your voices be heard in the marketplace is to vote with your wallet. If any of the aforementioned data say anything then it is we are fighting with our wallets, but it is on a digital scale. Governments have always hated cash. This is now their chance to phase out physical Federal Reserve Notes, euros, and pounds and introduce digits.

The war on cash is not to be fought with bullets and bombs, debates and treaties. The war on cash is being fought with every swipe, tap, wave, heartbeat, and thumbprint.

Cash is dead. Long live cash!

Made in the USA
Coppell, TX
26 February 2021